Freedom Tide

Now You Can Make a Difference!

Chad Connelly

**Executive
Books**

To the man who inspired me to learn about and fight for free enterprise principles by teaching me how to be successful in a business of my own,

Billy Florence

To my Mom, Dorothy Connelly, who gave me my love for books by teaching me that they were my best friends.

And to my Dad, Bruce Connelly, who has told me all my life that I could do anything I put my mind to if I wanted it badly enough.

Freedom Tide

Published by
Executive Books
206 West Allen Street
Mechanicsburg, PA 17055

ISBN: 0-937539-68-6

LCCN: 2002108043

Printed in the United States of America

Cover design by David M. Bullock/Susquehanna Direct

04   5 4 3

Contents

Contents

Introduction

In 1992, William J. Bennett, Secretary of Education under Ronald Reagan, wrote *The Index of Leading Cultural Indicators*, the most comprehensive statistical picture available of trends from 1960 through 1990. In this thirty-year span, according to the *Index*,

> ...there has been a 560 percent increase in violent crime, more than a 400 percent increase in illegitimate births, a quadrupling in divorces, a tripling of percentages of children living in single-parent homes, more than a 200 percent increase in the teenage suicide rate, and a drop of almost 80 points in the average SAT scores of high school students. The empirical evidence is clear. During the last three decades, American society has experienced substantial social regression.

A 2000 update of the *Index* added that the number of prisoners in state and federal prisons is up 463% in the last forty years; out of wedlock births now account for 32% of births nationally, 26% of all pregnancies are aborted, and the television is now on in the American household for an average of seven hours and twelve minutes per day."[1]

What has happened to us? What could possibly cause such sharp and dangerous declines in key areas of American society? This book may not have all of the answers, but it points out some likely culprits, and one in particular: an amazing lack of recognition of God's providential hand on our country. We no longer have knowledge of, or respect for, the history and beliefs that made America the envy of the world. Worse, our ignorance and inaction have actually enabled our freedoms to erode—and freedoms, once lost, are not easily regained.

But more importantly, this book is a call to action; a challenge to blaze a trail that will return our country to its founding principles before it's too late. Rabbi Daniel Lapin said it best in his book *America's Real War*: "I seek to encourage those Americans similarly inclined to help return America to its founding moral imperative. This is neither a cry for religious revolution nor a crusade; it is something else entirely. It is a reminder that we have lost our way. It is a suggestion that we return home again."[2]

We are looking for those of you out there who know you feel this way but never thought that your efforts could matter. They do. Change has always begun with a groundswell from the people. Grass roots involvement and activism have always made a difference. We can put our hearts and minds together and restore our nation to its greatest glory. Let there be no doubt: the tide of the future is a *Freedom Tide!*

I have often said that the tide of the future is a freedom tide. If so, it is also a peace tide, for the surest guarantee we have of peace is national freedom and democratic government.

—Ronald Reagan

Chapter 1

Why am I Here?

With the exception of the 1941 attack on Pearl Harbor, Americans had enjoyed almost 189 years of peace from foreign attack on their own soil until September 11, 2001. Just as Pearl Harbor left an indelible impression on our forefathers, we will never forget the nightmarish scenes of terrorists using our own jumbo jets as missiles to demolish some of the most cherished monuments to our nation's success. As always, Americans rose to the occasion: blood banks were swamped with donations; the Red Cross and other charities saw unprecedented levels of giving. Ordinary people became heroes as they sacrificed their safety to help others as buildings crumbled around them.

The attacks left many Americans scratching their heads and wondering, "What happened? How could this have happened to us?" Now, as we face a new war like none we have ever experienced, it appears that our nation is returning to some of the basic roots of its greatness. A patriotic wave of unity has swept through the country. American flags have become the hottest commodity in the land, professional sports games are being delayed so that the players and fans can see newscasts of President George W. Bush speaking to the nation, and "God Bless America" is being sung with a new depth of emotion. On a fall trip through the Northeast, our family even saw Massachusetts Department of Transportation signs with the flashing message "God Bless America!"

This is the perfect time for reflection. Now is the time for asking ourselves some hard questions. People everywhere have discovered that they can make a difference and that a life of plain existence does not benefit many people. Pictures of ordinary Americans pitching in to help in so many different ways has motivated even more people to get involved. What if we could *all* make a decision to make more of a difference in the lives of others instead of just rolling through life? That was the question I asked myself as I began my career right out of Clemson University in 1985.

* *

Like most 22-year-olds, I was excited about graduation and the start of "real life." As I sat on an old wooden bench shaded by a sprawling oak tree overlooking a vast, green expanse known as Bowman Field with Michelle, the beautiful blonde I had fallen in love with, I told her of my dreams to "just make a difference" in this world. I was frustrated that I had been so involved in college and couldn't really see that my efforts had any long-term effect. At some point in life most of us come to the crossroads where we ask the questions, "Why am I here and what am I supposed to do with my life?" Those questions swirled around in my brain as I faced college graduation, marriage, and my first "real" job. As I held her hand and talked about life, it occurred to me that, now that I had graduated from college, I had an empty feeling. I felt that the impact I had made in college was akin to putting my fist in a bucket of water, pulling it out, and the hole that was left was the sum total of the difference I had made. It was depressing to think about.

I had mapped out a career as a civil engineer with a large engineering firm, and Michelle had dreams of traveling the world working for a bank. We planned on being loyal company employees, riding up the corporate ladder and following the path prescribed for "success." Little did we know that within three short years our desire to make a difference would lead us to starting our own business.

At a point when my young engineering career was beginning to soar, my Dad was downsized from a corporation that he had worked for for over twenty years. The week before Christmas he was called in and told, "Thanks for your twenty years of service, but we don't need you anymore." Needless to say, the news crushed him and our family. Since my Dad has always been my best friend and hero, I was also deeply hurt and somewhat disillusioned about a corporate career. I determined that I would not be subject to a boss who could ever say to me "See ya bud, we don't need you anymore."

A few years after Michelle and I got married, a business acquaintance and good friend approached me about partnering with him in a business of our own. It was then that my life started to change. Even though my Dad was a successful salesman and had taught me many success principles, I started learning about what seems to be a foreign term in our world today: *free enterprise*. I am not sure I could have even defined the meaning of these two words that have set our country apart. Webster's says that *free enterprise* is a practice of permitting private industry to operate under freely competitive conditions with a minimum of government control. Free enterprise was a dream of our country's founders, but I am not so sure our present and future are dedicated to that ideal.

We live in a world of choices. Whether we are just starting out in life or have come to a point of starting over, we have some choices to make. Each of us has to make a choice about our philosophy, what we believe in and why we believe it. In today's America, there is confusion about what people believe in and why. A short analysis of our economic choices and our history clears up most of the confusion.

Our country proudly boasts of our freedoms. The freedoms we enjoy have come at a price but the principles of free enterprise have allowed our people to succeed with a minimum of government interference. The extreme alternative to free enterprise is communism. In the second half of the twentieth century, the primary world conflict was between free enterprise, with its individual freedoms, and communism and government control—fundamentally different ideologies that formed the foundation of the Cold War.

Communism is the government control of the tools of production. It is an economic system based on state ownership of all property where equal distribution of goods is achieved by revolutionary or dictatorial means rather than by gradual means. In other words, the state is running and planning an economy where the government controls the tools of production and distribution in contrast to a system where individuals carry out production and distribution through free enterprise and guaranteed individual liberties.

Today, you cannot find many people who identify themselves as communist, but you do hear a lot about another political philosophy called socialism. Socialism is an incremental step between free enterprise and communism, but, like communism, it is a system in which private ownership of the means of production is limited by the state.

As a freshman at Clemson in 1981, I experienced the patriotic wave that President Ronald Reagan brought to America. The country was recovering from an unpopular war in Vietnam, which, coupled with sky-high interest rates and inflation, brought the country's patriotism to a low ebb. I joined Army ROTC and I vividly remember the transition from being laughed at around campus to being applauded as President Reagan's message of free enterprise and patriotism took hold. I was proud to wear our country's uniform and I knew where I stood on issues. Late night discussions in the fraternity house always seemed to be about who we were, what our destiny was, and what we believed in.

When I entered the corporate world, my beliefs and dreams were suppressed because the popular mantra was—and is—"do not talk about religion and politics." You know—don't offend anyone, don't step on people's toes. Be politically correct. A good friend of mine once said, "If you don't talk about religion and politics, then you are going to end up voting for someone who doesn't believe in what you believe in and they will end up legislating you right out of business."

If you don't know where you stand on religious and moral issues, you develop what I refer to as a "sliding scale of absolutes." An absolute is an unchanging standard. Webster's defines absolute as "free from imperfection, perfect, pure, fundamental, ultimate, having no exception or qualification." It is sad that many have adopted the standard of not *having* any real standard. The experts today call this "situational ethics." That's a broad term that means you define right and wrong based on the current situation. When people run into a standard that they don't like, they slide the scale to fit their behavior and absolute truths are replaced or distorted. On *The O'Reilly Factor*, televised on Fox News on May 15, 2001, CBS News Anchor Dan Rather explained why he believes Bill Clinton is an upright man. "I think you can be an honest person and lie about any number of things."[3] How's that for a sliding scale?

I recently read an analogy that describes this scenario well. Let's suppose that you and I are in a sailboat rolling with the waves across the sea. Imagine that we are having a discussion about our navigational methods. I tell you that we aren't progressing and that I can't tell if your methods are working even though you are navigating by the fixed stars in the night sky. So I determine to navigate by the light on the top of our boat's mast. This is logical, isn't it? It's situational, right? After all, that light is brighter and closer to us, I argue. The problem, you respond, is that the light on top of our boat's mast is moving! Worse than that, it moves with *us*: thus our entire frame of reference isn't fixed; it's in constant motion! The real problem in our scenario is obvious. By the fixed stars, anyone can navigate successfully; but, by the light on the mast, no one can navigate at all. It sure seems like a lot of people in our world today are attempting to navigate their lives with "sliding scales" of absolutes, or by the mast light on top of their own masts. Can anyone deny that our country has experienced massive moral decay, social problems, and a general confusion of what's right and what's wrong? The whole world recognizes America as the beacon of the world. America is the greatest country in the world: our wealth, our standard of living, our productivity, and our free enterprise are the envy of all. What made our country great, and why? Can we sustain its greatness for our children's children? Do the standards and absolutes established at our founding have anything to do with our greatness?

The cause of America is in a great measure the cause of all mankind. Where, say some, is the King of America? I'll tell you friend; He reigns above.

—Thomas Paine

Chapter 2

Chance or Providence?

In his speech to a joint session of Congress on September 20, 2001, President George W. Bush said, "Terrorists attacked a *symbol* of American prosperity. They did not touch its *source*. America is successful because of the hard work and creativity and enterprise of our people."[4] President Bush is totally correct. America's strength is, and always has been, her people. The free enterprise system could have developed only in America. No other government in history has given individuals the right to succeed or fail on their own efforts. The individuals who first drove that thinking are responsible for placing the foundation blocks in the structure of what has become the greatest country in the world. But a building is only as strong as its foundation. Over time, if that foundation is not maintained, it will erode. I believe the founding principles of our country have been covered up, glossed over, made a mockery of, and basically reinterpreted over the last generation. Our principles have eroded. We need to return to those original principles that made our country what it is today—before it is too late. Critics say, "We don't really know what the founders thought," so I did a little research. I found we do know what the founders thought because they wrote it down. They wrote and wrote and wrote. Ignoring all of this documentation, the cornerstones of America have been distorted and changed to meet the "political correctness" of the day. In an attempt to be inoffensive and politically correct, many people have watered down our beliefs and values. Television talk show host and author Bill O'Reilly said, "There is a point where political correctness becomes an acid that erodes freedom."[5]

Nowadays, it seems that many of us don't know our own history. A popular segment of *The Tonight Show* has host Jay Leno going to the streets to interview people about our history. The audience laughs at their incorrect answers and lack of knowledge, but those citizens highlight the tragic truth that our founding principles and heritage have been lost. People assume that they learned all they needed to know in school and very few pick up a book to read the real story.

A couple of years ago, Michelle and I traveled with some business leaders to Plymouth, Massachusetts. Local friends had advised us to skip it because "It's just a rock." Going to Plymouth, however, turned out to be one of the most exciting and life-changing trips I have ever taken. What made this so impactful was that Marshall Foster, a leading Christian historian specializing in America's founding, led our group. Plymouth is definitely more than "just a rock" to Marshall. We stood at William Bradford's gravesite on the hill overlooking Plymouth Rock and listened with awe. Marshall wept as he related stories of the Pilgrim's hardships, struggles, and sacrifices. In all my years of schooling, I had never heard most of the stories he described. I certainly had never bothered to read the actual accounts of the day.

Marshall told us how the Pilgrims landed in

November 1620, spending two weeks aboard ship without disembarking, praising and giving glory to God while they wrote out a document called the Mayflower Compact which explained their incursion to this New World.

> Having undertaken, for the glory of God and advancement of the Christian faith and honor of our king and country, a voyage to plant the first colony ...[6]

The Pilgrims left no doubt as to why they had come here. The Mayflower Compact held sacred the same principles of equality of all men and government by the people that would subsequently become the foundational principles of the American system of self-government. This agreement marked the first time in recorded history that free and equal men had voluntarily covenanted together to create their own new civil government.

One hundred two people were on the trip to Plymouth. They had courage and faith. They climbed aboard a ship in 1620 on the faith that the boat was going to go to a new land located somewhere to the west of them. I always thought that many Pilgrims died on the trip. Marshall taught us that only one person died during the seven-week trip—a sailor who cursed and mocked the Pilgrim's efforts died of a mysterious disease that no one else caught. Moreover, a baby was born during the voyage. During the trip, the huge crossbeam supporting the main mast broke in the midst of a violent storm. The captain and crew were certain that the ship could not take any more thrashing and would soon sink. The Pilgrims didn't know how to help, so they gathered around the mast and prayed. As they prayed, William Brewster remembered the huge iron screw of his printing press. The screw was found in the ship's hold and cranked into place, raising the beam back to its original position and allowing the Pilgrims to complete the trip to the New World. This was one of the first of many miracles that the Pilgrims experienced.

The Pilgrims arrived in the New World only to endure a horrific winter. Of the twenty women who made the journey fifteen perished that first winter, mostly as they covered their children from the cold and gave up their food so their children could survive. Food was so sparse that the daily allotment per person was five kernels of corn a day. Want a surefire way of discouraging your family from descending upon your home for Thanksgiving? Just reenact the first winter at Plymouth. A couple of years ago I had my family over for Thanksgiving. We had all of the good stuff cooking in the background—the turkey, the pies, the dressing, cakes and everything else. We went into the next room to say our prayer. I had them hold out their hands and I put five kernels of corn in each. I told the story of the Pilgrims and their plight that first winter in America. I believe it impacted them as much as it had me when I heard this story from Marshall. Those mothers sacrificed their lives for the future: despite the loss of fifteen women, not a single child died during the first winter. Another amazing miracle.

William Bradford was elected the Pilgrim's governor. He decided that every man needed his own plot of land. The group had tried to work a socialist system where everybody worked on the community farm. There was no incentive to succeed because not everyone would work equally. Bradford's answer was to give each family a plot of land. He told them it was their individual right to succeed or to fail. Free enterprise was born because whoever did the best decided to do the best because they decided to work the hardest for their own profit.

What all this told me was that the Pilgrims started something special in America—with their sacrifices they lit a freedom fire that has burned brightly for over 380 years. Even with all of our problems, America still has the best form of government in the world. People come from all over the world to see what makes our country special. The Pilgrims with their faith and courage lit a little flame that people today will still die to reach. Stories of Americans tearing their homes apart to build a boat to escape our freedoms are unheard of; however, similar stories of immigrants coming here and risking their lives are numerous even though they hardly even make the news anymore.

The time we spent in the Pilgrim graveyard with Marshall and our friends was overwhelming. We saw other things that I'm sure the regular tour doesn't include: burial sites, the women's monument dedicated to the sacrifices they made to save their children, and the greatest monument detailing the Christian founding of America. That monument, called the Founder's Monument (or the Forefather's Monument on local tourist maps), was designed to remind everyone of the Pilgrim ideals of faith, morality, education, law, and justice. When William Bradford became governor he dedicated this land to the God of Heaven. Under his leadership, the people prayed, fasted and succeeded with their plots of land. To this day, some 380 years later, America has not experienced a famine. We have heard of famines all over the world, but we have not had a nationwide famine since our founding. We have been bountifully and miraculously blessed. Not by accident, but by providence. William Bradford probably best summed up the Pilgrims' settlement in the New World in his history, *Of Plymouth Plantation*, when he said,

> Thus out of small beginnings greater things have been pro-
> duced by His hand that made all things of nothing, and gives
> being to all things that are; and, as one small candle may
> light thousands, so the light here kindled hath shone unto
> many, yea, in some sort to our whole nation; let the glorious
> name of Jehovah have all the praise.[7]

America's Founding Fathers went on to give us our system of government—a republic. It has enjoyed unprecedented success. We have flourished for over 225 years under one document. If you want to know how impressive a single unchanged form of government is, just look at France: in the last two hundred years, France has had seven completely different forms of government. Italy is on its 51st form of government in 225 years. Obviously, our foundational principles have led to unparalleled stability. Since there are no other examples of freedom in this age lasting this long, no one can claim it is by chance. The Founding Fathers gave us a document called the *Constitution*. It is described today as a "living, breathing document." I believe that's meant to say that the Constitution is timeless. It wasn't written so magnificently that it has endured so long because the founders were so smart. I believe that it was providentially, divinely appointed. There is no other explanation for the magnitude and wisdom of our founding documents. The results of our long-standing freedoms compared with those of other nations speak for themselves. So, what has made America special and the idea called "freedom" so different?

I shall need, too, the favor of that Being in whose hands we are, who led our fathers, as Israel of old, from their land and planted them in a country flowing with all the necessaries and comforts of life; who has covered our infancy with His providence and our riper years with His wisdom and power.

—Thomas Jefferson

Chapter 3

What Did the Founders Say?

There exist today two schools of thought on the Constitution. One school could be described as the liberal view that holds a broad or changing interpretation of what the Founders intended. This is the *loose constructionist* interpretation. The other is the conservative view that believes the Founders meant exactly what they said in the Constitution. This is the *strict constructionist* interpretation. Liberal thought defines "living breathing document" as meaning you can change and massage the Constitution and make it say whatever you want it to—the sliding scale of absolutes again. For example, the Fourteenth Amendment, ratified in 1868, had the fundamental aim of preventing the Southern (ex-Confederate) states from denying basic rights and freedoms to their former slaves. Yet in the twentieth century, a liberal-influenced Supreme Court used the Fourteenth Amendment to ban prayer, Bible reading, and the posting of the Ten Commandments in our state-run public school systems. The problem is, who determines the absolute? If you are in power, then **you** get to decide, and the people have to contend with a flexible, man-inspired idea of absolute. Let's go back to the example of the sailboat and the mast. Imagine that your leaders decide that they must determine all absolutes. When this happens, everyone has to discuss the meaning of the word "is" as illustrated by a recent president when confronted with his interpretation of the truth. The Constitution was written to be timeless—"living and breathing." But I also believe it was divinely appointed so that no man or group could just come into power and change it based on their own beliefs or the prevailing beliefs of the time. When all the people have rules but the hierarchy does not, then tyranny reigns. Throughout history, this is what we have seen all over the world.

John Jay was our original Chief Justice. He would have known about the Constitution and its intended meaning. He said, "Providence has given our people the choice of their rulers. It is the duty as well as the privilege and interest of our Christian nation to select and prefer Christians for their rulers."[8] Today's constitutional experts do not seem to quote the first Chief Justice of the United States. You have heard them quote the Chief Justice who ended prayer in schools, but you haven't heard them quote the Chief Justice who was there when the founders discussed the reasons for writing what they did.

Another great example is George Washington's Farewell Address. "Of all the dispositions and habits that lead to political prosperity," Washington said, "religion and morality are indispensable supports."[9] (*Indispensable* does not mean *optional*.) Washington's words were in nearly every American history text until 1965. *Since* 1965 it has not appeared in a single one. With quotes like this scrubbed out of our schoolbooks, it's no wonder many who live in the United States don't know their own country's heritage. Just think, the Father of our Country, who was a member of the original Continental Congress, who helped draft the founding documents, who led our troops in the American

Revolution, and who served two terms as our nation's President, in his last public statement said that religion and morality are indispensable supports. With all that experience, effort, sacrifice and service, George Washington would *have* to be the most uniquely qualified individual in history to know what it takes for a nation to prosper!

David Barton of WallBuilders, an organization dedicated to the restoration of the moral and religious foundation on which America was built, wrote that the University of Houston actually assembled 15,000 writings of the Founding Fathers. Researchers isolated 3,154 direct quotes and the Bible was quoted four times more than anything else. The Founding Fathers quoted John Locke, Montesquieu and Sir William Blackstone—people who were great thinkers, philosophers and writers of their day. But thirty-four percent of the quotes came directly from the Bible. We **do** know what they said, what they thought and what they believed because they wrote it down. Thomas Jefferson was not known as the most Christian of the founders, but even *he* believed the Bible ought to be read in schools. While President of the United States, Jefferson chaired the school board for the District of Columbia and authored its plan of education using the Bible and Watt's *Hymnal* as reading texts.[10]

Patrick Henry, known as the Trumpet of the Revolution, was attributed with saying, "It cannot be emphasized too strongly or too often that this great nation was founded not by religionists but by Christians—not on religion, but on the gospel of Jesus Christ".[11]

"It is the duty of all nations to acknowledge the providence of Almighty God, to obey His will, to be grateful for His benefits, and to humbly implore His protection and favor."[12] This was George Washington on October 3, 1789, proclaiming a National Day of Prayer and Thanksgiving.

Noah Webster, one of the founders and the author of our first dictionary, wrote in his 1832 *History of the United States*: "The moral principles and concepts contained in the Scriptures ought to form the basis of all our civil constitutions and laws... All the miseries and evils which man may suffer from vice, crime, ambition, injustice, oppression, slavery and war, proceed from their despising or neglecting the precepts contained in the Bible."[13]

James Madison, the fourth President of the United States, is credited with the quote, "We have staked the whole future of American civilization not on the power of government, far from it, we have staked the future of all of our political institutions upon the capacity of each and all of us to govern ourselves according to the Ten Commandments of God".[14]

You may have seen the next quote. It is engraved in the stone monument on the Jefferson Memorial in Washington, D.C.: "God who gave us life gave us liberty. And can the liberties of a nation be thought secure when we have removed their only firm basis, a conviction in the minds of the people that these liberties are a gift of God? That they are not to be violated but with His wrath? Indeed, I tremble for my country when I reflect that God is just; that His justice cannot sleep forever."[15] Kind of sounds like a Billy Graham quote I heard not too long ago: "If God doesn't soon punish America, he will have to apologize to Sodom and Gomorrah."

Another convincing statement came from Benjamin Franklin at the Constitutional Convention on June 28, 1787: "We have been assured, Sir, in the sacred writings, that 'except the Lord build the house, they labor in vain that build it.' I firmly believe this; and I also believe that without His concurring aid we shall succeed in this political building no better than the builders of Babel... I therefore beg leave to move, that henceforth, prayers imploring the assistance of Heaven and its blessings on our deliberations, be held in this assembly every morning before we proceed to business, and that one or more of the clergy of this city be requested to officiate in that service."[16]

George Washington said, while addressing the General Committee representing the United Baptist Churches of Virginia on May 10, 1789, "If I could have entertained the slightest apprehension that the constitution which was framed in our convention where I had the honor to preside, might possibly endanger the religious rights of any ecclesiastical society, certainly I would have never placed my signature on it."[17] In today's vernacular we would say, "I wouldn't have signed it if I thought it would have threatened any expression of religion."

Can we seriously question what the founders believed and whether or not they constructed the foundation of our government on the sound and solid principles found in the Bible? In addition to the individual founders' words, official government bodies also did not hesitate to declare their views. The Maryland Supreme Court in 1799 stated unanimously, "Religion is of general and public concern and on its support depend, in great measure, the peace and good order of government, the safety and happiness of the people. By our form of government, the Christian religion is the established religion; and all sects and denominations of Christians are placed on the same equal footing and are equally entitled to protection in their religious liberty."[18]

In 1854 a United States House of Representatives Judiciary Committee report added, "Had the people during the Revolution had a suspicion of any attempt to war against Christianity, that Revolution would have been strangled in its cradle. At the time of the constitution and the amendments, the universal sentiment was that Christianity should be encouraged, but not any one denomination. Any attempt to level and discard all religion would have been viewed with universal indignation... It [religion] must be considered as the foundation on which the whole structure rests... In this age there can be no substitute for Christianity... That was the religion of the founders of the republic, and they expected it to remain the religion of their descendants."[19]

I pray that you might obtain that knowledge which is reserved for babes and the simple-minded, while it is hid from the wise and prudent.

—François Fénelon

Chapter 4

What Does the First Amendment Say?

Probably the most prominent example of the freedom debate is the controversy over the First Amendment. Some believe that it guarantees the separation of church and state. This seems to be one of the most divisive issues in America today, and many people have succumbed to the media's interpretation without ever checking out the truth for themselves. Here are some truths for us to ponder: the words "wall," "separation," "church" or "state" are not found in any of America's founding documents In fact, in the months of discussion of the First Amendment in the Constitutional Convention, not one of the ninety founders who participated ever mentioned the phrase "separation of church and state."[20]

These words ARE found in a document, but the document is Article 124 of the Constitution of the former Soviet Union. "The church in the USSR is separated from the state and the school from the church."[21] This same concept is also expressed in the United Nations charter. Isn't it amazing that the majority of Americans are convinced that this phrase originated with our Founding Fathers?

Here's what the First Amendment actually states:

33

"Congress shall make no law respecting an establishment of religion or prohibiting the free exercise thereof; or abridging the freedom of speech, or of the press; or the right of the people peaceably to assemble and to petition the Government for a redress of grievances." CONGRESS shall make no law. Notice that there is no reference to what a church or a pastor or a student in school or a school principal shall not do. It refers only to restrictions placed on Congress. It doesn't say that a child cannot pray in school or that a nativity scene cannot be displayed on public property. It only restrains the *federal government from infringing on the religious freedoms* of the American people. Today that has been subverted to mean that the Supreme Court using the Fourteenth Amendment can even interpret that various instances of worship violate the Constitution!

James Madison, who was the chief architect of the Constitution and our fourth President, in discussions on the First Amendment, proposed, "The civil rights of none shall be abridged on account of religious belief or worship, nor shall any national religion be established".[22]

Clearly, the founders wanted to insure that Godly principles were established as our country's foundation. They were not attempting to exclude any religion. Their forefathers had endured a state established religion in England. America's founders learned that lesson and wanted to give freedom to all, but they also knew that a country founded without Godly principles and absolutes would not survive long term. "The people of a free nation must have a foundation that will support liberty, for without it, that nation will surely fall." The great Nineteenth Century statesman and politician Daniel Webster spoke these words at the bicentennial celebration of the landing of the Pilgrims at Plymouth Rock, December 22, 1820: "If we and our posterity shall be true to the Christian religion, if we and they shall always live in the fear of God and shall respect His commandments,… we may have the highest hopes of the future fortunes of our country;… But if we and our posterity neglect religious instruction and authority, violate the rules of eternal justice, trifle with the injunctions of morality, and recklessly destroy the political constitution which holds us together, no man can tell us how sudden a catastrophe may overwhelm us that shall bury all our glory in profound obscurity."[23]

The debate about our founders' intentions and where we stand today makes us question: what changed and when? William James, the father of modern psychology, said, "There is nothing so absurd, but if you repeat it enough people will believe it."[24] Adolf Hitler, like James, recognized the power of repetition in getting people to believe lies. "The ultimate in Hitlerian propaganda technique is the principle of the big lie. Hitler declared '…that the very greatness of the lie is a factor in getting it believed… a great lie is more effective than a small one….' In brief, the bigger the lie, the more likely it will be believed by the masses."[25]

Similarly, the Supreme Court and the mainstream media have used that technique so successfully that the bulk of the American people have become convinced that the Constitution and the Founding Fathers favored removal of religion from both education and government. Nothing could be further from the truth. In fact, in a dissenting opinion in a 1958 case, *Baer v. Kolmorgen*, Supreme Court Justice Gallagher wrote, "Much has been written in recent years… to a 'wall of separation between church and state'…[It] has received so much attention that one would almost think at times that it is to be found somewhere in our Constitution."[26]

I submit that our moral and social decay is linked to our citizens' indifference and failure to investigate the facts. It certainly appears that many today are trying to guide their boats and everyone else's by that light on top of the mast. It doesn't take a deep reading of the actual Founders' words to realize that they knew this country's basis and successful future were both determined by absolute navigation, not by a changing standard.

David Barton of WallBuilders has compiled what is probably one of the most exhaustive studies on the First Amendment issue. He has written several entire books on the subject, but his research is well summarized in the video and book, *America's Godly Heritage*. Barton discusses a number of challenges to our Christian roots brought before the Supreme Court in the Nineteenth Century. In each one, the Supreme Court ruled in favor of keeping Biblical principles as one of the pillars of our society, according to the founder's intentions.[27] For example, in 1844, a Philadelphia school announced that it would teach morality to its students, but not religion. It believed it didn't need Christianity and the Bible to teach morality. Sounds a lot like today's "modern" approach. The Philadelphia policy caused a suit that reached the Supreme Court. The Court told the school:

> Why may not the Bible, and especially the New Testament... be read and taught as a divine revelation in the [school]—its general precepts expounded... and its glorious principles of morality inculcated? Where can the purest principles of morality be learned so clearly or so perfectly as from the New Testament?[28]

In 1892, the Supreme Court stated in *Church of the*

Holy Trinity vs. U.S.: "No purpose of action against religion can be imputed to any legislation, state or national, because this is a religious people... This is a Christian nation."[29] In this case, the Court actually used 87 different historical precedents to support its conclusions. The Court quoted the Founding Fathers, the acts of the Founding Fathers, the acts of different Congresses, and the acts of state governments. At the end of the 87 precedents, the Court explained that it could continue to cite many more, but that certainly 87 were sufficient to conclude that we were a Christian nation.[30]

The Twentieth Century produced a dramatic shift in the court's thinking. Influenced by a reassessment of the role of religion in society by some leading intellectuals, the Supreme Court began to view the separation of church and state as a means of keeping non-believers from possibly being tainted by "state-sponsored" religious activities. Suddenly, religion was no longer an indispensable foundation of American society; it was now viewed as a reactionary obstacle to secular progress. Secularists, who saw the necessity of eliminating religion as an influence on public institutions, applauded the "wall of separation" doctrine as expressed in *Everson v. Board of Education* (1947).[31]

Religion was now the foremost symbol of everything that was wrong in American society. While the majority of Americans continued to believe in God and country, the intellectuals, aided by an activist and liberal Supreme Court, moved toward their goal of relegating religion to the heart, the home and the church. In *Everson*, the Supreme Court stated that the government—both federal and state—must be neutral, not just between groups of Protestants but between Protestants and non-Protestants and believers and non-believers. This interpretation of government neutrality flies against the intentions of the Founding Fathers as well as over one hundred and fifty years of judicial rulings and interpretations.

The Court also set forth—for the first time—the "wall of separation" doctrine which in the last fifty years has been interpreted increasingly more liberally. In the words of Justice Hugo Black, "The First Amendment has erected a wall between church and state. That wall must be kept high and impregnable. We could not approve the slightest breech."[32] In creating the "wall of separation" doctrine, the Court relied on a private letter that Thomas Jefferson wrote in 1802 to the Danbury Baptists. The Danbury Baptist Association of Danbury, Connecticut, which had experienced severe persecution for its faith, wrote President Jefferson asking what the term "free exercise of religion," as it appeared in the First Amendment, meant. To the Danbury Baptists, the free exercise of religion meant, according to Barton, "...that the right to religious exercise was a government-granted rather than a God-granted, right, thus implying that someday government might try to regulate religious expression. They believed that freedom of religion was given by God, an inalienable right, and that the government should be powerless to restrict religious activities..."[33]

In reassuring the Danbury Baptists that the First Amendment simply prevented the Federal establishment of a single state denomination, like the Anglican Church in England, Jefferson wrote:

> Believing with you that religion is a matter which lies solely between man and his God, that he owes account to none other for faith or his worship, that the legislative powers of government reach actions only, and not opinions, I contem-

plate with solemn reverence that act of the whole American people which declared that their legislature should make no law respecting an establishment of religion, or prohibiting the free exercise thereof, thus building a wall between church and state.[34]

This private letter calmed the Baptists' fears that the government could not control or interfere with the decisions and affairs of America's churches. It should be noted that Thomas Jefferson *did not* sign the Constitution and was not in attendance at the Constitutional Convention in 1787. Not only that, but he was *not even present* when the First Amendment and religious freedom were discussed in the 1789 Constitutional session since he was in France as a United States Minister.[35]

The Court, in *Everson*, took Jefferson's letter out of context, thus rejecting the historical root of Christianity in America and establishing a guideline by which future cases further restricted many people's right to freedom of religion.

The First Amendment was never intended to wall off Christianity or religion in government but rather to guarantee that a national church would never be established. The founders knew the kind of state religions that had been established in Europe and did not want to repeat those mistakes. For over one hundred and fifty years the Supreme Court understood that the First Amendment simply prohibited the establishment of a single state appointed denomination.

The importance of the *Everson* case was that the Supreme Court lifted only eight words: "...a wall of separation between church and state..." from Jefferson's letter to create a new church-state doctrine. *Everson* also extended the prohibitions of the First Amendment to the states through the Fourteenth Amendment—another instance of the Supreme Court's stretching the original intent of an amendment far beyond what the framers intended. Instead of standing firm on the principles and values of the Founding Fathers, the Court was watching societal trends and reacting accordingly. *Everson* radically altered the original intent of the First Amendment as another founding absolute started sliding to accommodate the new secularization of America.

Remember, in our brief view of the founders' words, our Founding Fathers relied on the Bible, early text books quoted the Bible, schools used the Bible to teach the alphabet, and the Supreme Court ruled that a school must teach religion and the Bible. The founders had a natural yearning to remove obstacles to freedom and to acknowledge God. Their faith permeated everything they did, and they knew that to remove it would invite destruction.

James Madison, in his Presidential Proclamation in 1815, said, "Before any man can be considered a member of civil society, he must be considered as a subject of the Governor of the Universe."[36] Benjamin Rush (1745-1813), one of the youngest signers of the Declaration of Independence said, "Let the children... be carefully instructed in the principles and obligations of the Christian religion. This is the most essential part of education. The great enemy of the salvation of man, in my opinion, never invented a more effectual means of extirpating (removing) Christianity from the world than by persuading mankind that it was improper to read the Bible at schools."[37]

Even present Chief Justice William Rehnquist, as have a number of justices before him, disagrees with the court's rewriting of history in the *Everson* decision. Rehnquist said, "But the greatest injury of the 'wall' notice is its mischievous diversion of judges from the actual intentions of the drafters of the Bill of Rights... The 'wall of separation between church and state' is a metaphor based on bad history, a metaphor which has proved useless as a guide to judging. It should be frankly and explicitly abandoned."[38]

Following the precedent set in the Everson case, The Supreme Court during the Earl Warren era progressively moved to cleanse the public institutions of America of the influences of Christianity. In *Engle v. Vitale* (1962), the Court outlawed school prayer. Justice Black, writing for the majority again, said:

> Who does not see that the same authority which can establish Christianity, in exclusion of all other religions, may establish with the same ease any particular sect of Christians, in exclusion of all other sects?[39]

Justice William O. Douglas, in a concurring opinion, stated:

> ...The philosophy is that the atheist or agnostic—the non-believer—is entitled to go his own way. The philosophy is that, if government interferes in matters spiritual, it will be a divisive force.[40]

To the Court, government "neutrality" meant no public institution could allow Christian prayer. This led to later rulings that forbade other public activities the Court deemed as religious.

The sliding scale of absolutes continued to move toward secularization in *Abington v. Schempp* in which the Court ruled that the voluntary reading of the Bible was unconstitutional. The Court's decision said:

> If portions of the New Testament were read without explana-
> tion, they could be and have been psychologically harmful to
> the child.[41]

What had been an indispensable part of our children's education since the founding of our nation suddenly
became "psychologically harmful." How can we as a nation
abandon our spiritual heritage just because we are handed a
new definition of freedom by the courts?

Once this trend of the public abandonment of
Christianity began, it continued in case after case. Still
ignoring almost 150 years of precedents, the Supreme Court
ruled in a Kentucky case, *Stone v. Graham*, that the Ten
Commandments could not be posted in schools.

> If the posted copies of the Ten Commandments are to have
> any effects at all, it will be to induce the school children to
> read, meditate upon, and perhaps to venerate and obey, the
> Commandments...[This] is not... a permissible... objec-
> tive.[42]

It is amazing to notice the difference in our
Founding Fathers' statements and the complete distortion of
them that is accepted as fact by today's courts and by many
of our citizens. Imagine that. Don't let kids read the Bible,
pray or see the Ten Commandments, but your friendly guidance counselor can give them condoms at the local public
school and some governments provide needles to drug
addicts for their use. Logically, why would some people be
opposed to schoolchildren reading statements like "don't
kill, don't steal, don't commit adultery?" No sane religion
in the world teaches that killing and stealing are permissi-
ble, and yet the Court said it didn't want to establish any
particular sect of religion. It makes you wonder if America
would have experienced the recent spate of school violence
and killing if our kids could simply see values like "Thou

Shalt Not Kill" reinforced instead of removed. Why have murder, violence, rape and other crimes skyrocketed? Could it be that the absolutes WERE taught at one time to our school children and then suddenly removed?

George Washington, in his Farewell Address, warned that "reason and experience both forbid us to expect that national morality can prevail in exclusion of religious principle."[43] We would have to agree that his warning has become prophetic. Critics say, "but it doesn't affect me." Maybe not, but teen pregnancy, drug abuse, rape, robbery, murder, school violence, pornography and other social ills scream at us from the front pages of newspapers every single day. Many people, who have clearly lost their way and are navigating with the light on their own boat, stand behind "freedom of speech and expression." Organized groups like the ACLU defend people in court and use Supreme Court cases to argue that these people are protected by "freedom of speech." In fact, the November 27, 2001 issue of *USA Today* chronicled the story of an ACLU lawyer who argued that the 1998 Child On-line Protection Act limits free speech. The act is designed to keep minors away from pornography on the Internet. It simply requires a website to collect credit card information or other adult ID as proof of age. It seems like common sense to most of us, but the ACLU says it violates the First Amendment. Are we to believe that Washington, Jefferson, Adams, Hamilton, and the other Founding Fathers would ever have considered online child pornography as "free speech?"

This is why it is so important for those of us who care to understand the truth, so that we are never fooled by the distortions. We need to stop the secularization of our public life and institutions and the sliding scale of absolutes that has made the redefining of our freedoms and values possible. How can that be accomplished? Where do we begin? One way we can make a difference is to respond to inaccuracies we find in the media about the First Amendment issue. Letters to the editors of local newspapers and phone calls and letters to local radio and TV stations not only serve to educate, but also have proven to be effective media of change. In the back of this book is a brief sample letter that may be used as a guideline for responding to people you read about or hear about who have adopted the "separation of church and state" misconception. What if one million letters like this were written and sent to local media outlets all across the country? Together, we can make a difference.

Government is not reason, it is not eloquence, it is force; like fire, a troublesome servant and a fearful master. Never for a moment should it be left to irresponsible action

—John Adams

Chapter 5

Liberal or Conservative: What Do They Mean?

In order to truly make a difference, we first have to decide where we stand on issues. I really did not know how I felt about some of the most relevant issues we face today until I started a business of my own. Being an independent business owner really made me think my true feelings through. It also exposed me to other successful business people who helped me shape my own thoughts.

In my corporate engineering career, most issues seemed to be suppressed or out of my area. I just did not have to confront anyone on them. Things were always handled by "corporate policy." As I built my own business, I encountered people every day who asked me what I thought or where I stood on everything from A to Z. I began to take a stand on many issues that people typically call controversial. But, if you don't stand for something, you will fall for anything. Ed Cole, founder of the Christian Men's Network, says it like this:

> Discovering principles is a lifelong passion for people who succeed. People who live by personality, preference or prejudice have no bedrock on which to build their lives and end up failing. Their foundation is shifting, moveable, unsteady. People who make decisions by personality or preference can be talked out of their decisions from one day to the next...

The more you build your life on principle, the higher your highs, the straighter your path, and the greater your life.[44]

It sure seems that many people today have tried to legislate morality right out of society and those efforts have cost our nation its moral standards. We now have many who want to live their lives by preference and not conviction. Have we become a people of immorality through natural circumstances, or has the change been purposeful?

There is a group of people in America that is concerned with the equality of opportunity. There is another group of people that is concerned with the equality of outcome. I believe that our founders wanted this to be a land of equal opportunity; they weren't looking for a handout. Equal opportunity dictates that each person has access to the same tools and the same resources. Each then chooses how hard to work based on how badly they want their goals and dreams. That is fairness. The other group proposes to legislate fairness by identifying people or groups of people who—in its view—don't have the same opportunity. This group constantly tries to level the playing field so that the *outcomes* are equal. Traditionally these views are known as liberal (*equality of outcome*) and conservative (*equality of opportunity*). I don't believe liberal versus conservative is a political party issue, although political parties can identify themselves as liberal or conservative. The issue is in our philosophy of life and in how these opposing viewpoints affect us. Again, it is imperative that we know what we believe and why.

"Conservatism... seeks to conserve the best elements of the past. Lincoln was once asked, "What is conservatism? Is it not adherence to the old and tried, against the new and untried?" His response: "It understands the important role that traditions, institutions, habits, and authority have in our social life together, and it recognizes many of our national institutions as products of principles developed over time by custom, the lessons of experience and consensus. Conservatives are interested in pursuing policies that will better reinforce and encourage the rest of our people's common culture, habits and beliefs. Conservatism, too, is based on the belief that the social order rests on a moral base..."[45]

Liberalism, on the other hand, implies tolerance to others' views as well as open mindedness to ideas that challenge tradition, even favoring progressive views that allow for fundamental or extreme change to traditional structure. I believe that an increasingly liberal view of government's role has led us to pull away from some of the traditions and principles upon which our country was founded.

Today's liberalism believes that the more government we have, the better. But, as government gets bigger, individuals inevitably lose freedoms. Liberals generally believe in more government instead of less, higher or increased taxes as opposed to lower taxes, weaker national defense and progressive family values instead of traditional family values. When taxes and regulation are increased, government has more power to control the people. Stronger central control in the hands of the government is the basic foundation of a socialistic or communistic state. It sounds so good in the short run, the idea that "government is going to help you... you need it." The implication is that you cannot succeed on your own without government help. Walter E. Williams, a free market economist and writer, described how government can easily slide into socialism by its very nature in a speech he gave at Hillsdale College.

The only way the government can give one American one dollar is to confiscate it first, under intimidation, threats, and coercion, from another American. In other words, for government to do good, it must first do evil. If a private person were to do the things that government does, he would be condemned as a common thief. The only difference is legality, and legality alone is no talisman for moral people. This reasoning explains why socialism is evil. It uses bad means (coercion) to achieve what are seen as good ends (helping people).[46]

The more dependent upon government we become, the *more* we are likely to want to become more dependent and the more we will give in to government's direction. Again, it all sounds so good and it's all done with apparent intentions of "helping people." In his book, *Mind Siege*, Tim LaHaye offers a scary statistic:

In 1920, approximately one government employee existed for every 100 citizens. Today, closer to one American in six works for the local, state, or federal government. The establishment of big government and its level of regulations has so eroded liberty that many experts fear we are well on our way to losing our traditional freedoms. For example, small business is being gradually choked by hostile regulations, mandatory procedures, punitive taxation... The federal government has become a kind of 'super' labor union.[47]

Bob McEwen, former Ohio Congressman and a noted free enterprise speaker, draws out the two different thought patterns like this:

<u>**European Model**</u>	<u>**Free Enterprise, or American Model**</u>
God	*God*
gives power to	gives power to
Government	*People*
which gives power to	who give power to
People	*Government*

The free enterprise model could be called "conservative" and the European model could be called "liberal." You often hear liberal politicians talk of "taxing the rich" because wealth and money are corrupt. They evidently believe that people who have become successful shouldn't keep more of their own money, or they may become corrupt. Liberals believe that more money should go to the government because government knows better how to spend your money than you do! It has always amazed me that the people who believe that money corrupts individuals couldn't see that individuals still make up the government. The only difference is that government did not earn the money—you did!

In addition to the liberal and conservative models, an ultra left has emerged over the past thirty years or so that believes that government gives power to the people with no recognition of any supreme creator. This belief was the basis for Karl Marx's *Communist Manifesto*. The government is supreme and everything is provided for you. There is no God. Many people are waking up and realizing that God and government aren't the same thing, and that government is made up of people.

All people are imperfect. Since people are imperfect, government is imperfect. Thus, when people have power without any moral direction, corruption is inevitable. The brilliance and foresight of our Founding Fathers can be seen in their firm reliance on a Supreme Being for guidance and direction. From the founders' faith and belief came the American experiment—capitalism and free enterprise.

The basis of capitalism and free enterprise is private property ownership. Karl Marx declared that the way to annihilate capitalism could be summarized in one phrase: "Abolition of private property."[48] The greatest private property ownership is not to own a car or a home, but to own and operate your own family business. Small businesses and independent business ownership drive America in that they give an individual a chance at the freedom to succeed or to fail in the marketplace. What better way to encourage individual liberty and responsibility than to have people working hard to become successful in a business of their own? The free market truly is the natural order of things.

Successful business owners are ones who look around their community, find a need, and fill it. Each business in a free market is rewarded in direct proportion to the service it provides to society. Its success is based primarily on its efforts and not on government intervention. Small business owners generally have a different attitude than most government organizations. If a government-run entity is losing money, the answer is to throw more money at the problem. For example, compare Federal Express, the overnight courier, with the postal service. While I admire and respect the postal workers' commitment and dedication, the organization embodies the inefficiency of government. There are some sixty-plus layers of management between the delivery person and the Postmaster General. On the other hand, there are less than ten layers of management between the FedEx delivery person and Fred Smith, the CEO. One organization reported a $1.7 billion loss and announced new price increases for first class stamps while the other, a multi-billion dollar enterprise, operates at a profit. A business owner who is losing money has to find ways to become more efficient or he has to close the business. That businessperson has to adapt and succeed on his own in the free market. He only becomes successful if he provides a quality product or service at a reasonable price to the public. In Milton Friedman's classic, *Free to Choose*, he says, "If the consumer is free to choose, an enterprise can grow in size only if it produces an item that the consumer prefers because of either its quality or price."[49]

Our Constitution was made only for a moral and religious people. It is wholly inadequate for the government of any other.

—John Adams

Proclaim liberty throughout all the land unto all the inhabitants thereof.

—Leviticus 25:10
Inscribed on the Liberty Bell

Chapter 6

Where Are We Now?

In order to keep our freedom strong, we all have to pitch in and do our part to make sure our way of life is preserved and continued. One of the greatest contributions to that end is to start and build a business of your own. Find a need and fill it. Find out where and how you can serve your fellow man. Author Gil Bailie, sharing some advice given to him by a spiritual mentor, better sums up this idea:

> Don't ask yourself what the world needs. Ask yourself what makes you come alive, and go do that, because what the world needs is people who have come alive.[50]

Strengthening our country's heritage is what makes me come alive. It makes me come alive with passion to make a difference and do something about our country's direction and future. Owning my own business has taught me that I am responsible for my family and myself. It has given me a unique insight into personal responsibility that I am sure I would not have gotten anywhere else. Our country could use a healthy dose of personal responsibility! We are going to believe that either people are capable or that the government is going to make them capable. I believe in the power of the individual to perform.

On December 4, 2001, President George W. Bush hosted a Town Hall meeting in Orlando, Florida. The discussion centered on the recent terrorist activity, the resulting war and the impact of those events on our economy. Several people who had lost jobs in the economic downturn asked, "What is government going to do for me?" President Bush answered that he was concerned about the job losses and explained that training programs and assistance were being made available. Then he added that in our land of free enterprise, it was not up to the government to determine your success or failure. That was up to each person. I really liked his answer. Personal responsibility and accountability are important aspects of our government. We have come to rely too much on the government for answers and solutions. Yes, there are times and situations when SOMEONE does have to step in and provide help. In the past, the community itself or the local church played substantial roles in assisting people. Today, many people expect the government to be the helping hand.

Former U.S. Representative Bob McEwen (Ohio) once explained the danger of a governmental helping hand:

> While governmental economic planning may sound attractive, it is fundamental that in order for a government social program to work we all must be fitted into it. Those who will not fit voluntarily are coerced. That is why they must build walls around socialist countries to keep people in to enjoy the benefits.[51]

I was in Venezuela recently speaking to a group about free enterprise. The people seemed very hungry to learn all that they could about our free market system, but many of them grew up and lived under some form of socialism. After the seminar, I had dinner with several business leaders who honestly asked about the differences between free enterprise and socialism. I answered by asking them what they thought government should provide for the people. They easily rattled off a list: housing, food, universal health care, welfare to the disadvantaged—all of which do sound attractive. They were just getting started when I asked how the government could afford to provide all of that. Then I decided to make the examples far-fetched to demonstrate that we would all love to have these things provided, but where do we draw the line? I asked if we could all have free cars, and if so, how big? What color? Two door or four door? I think they got the point. Where DO we draw the line? More importantly, WHO gets to decide where the line is drawn? We have to have clear thinking on these issues.

It's very easy to expect the government to always supply crutches for all the needs we could ever encounter. Either we are going to believe that people are capable of providing for themselves or we are going to believe that government will provide. That is why this is a philosophical question that each of us has to consider. Will I dedicate my life to principles that say people cannot provide for themselves and that government is all-powerful, or will I believe that individuals can succeed on their own? On one extreme is the totally humanistic and godless approach of communism that doesn't require morality because the government—the ones in power—decides what is right or wrong. On the other side is a free enterprise choice that requires people to take individual responsibility and is tied in to a set of absolute standards.

Sir Alexander Fraser Tyler described the consequences of ignoring this issue in his "Cycle of Nations" discussion in *The Decline and Fall of the Athenian Republic*:

A democracy cannot exist as a permanent form of government. It can only exist until the voters discover that they can vote themselves money from the public treasury. From that moment on, the majority always votes for the candidates promising the most benefits from the public treasury, with a result that a democracy always collapses over loose fiscal policy, always followed by dictatorship. The average age of the world's greatest civilizations has been 200 years. These nations have progressed through the following sequence:

- From bondage to spiritual faith
- From spiritual faith to great courage
- From courage to liberty
- From abundance to selfishness
- From selfishness to complacency
- From complacency to apathy
- From apathy to dependency
- From dependency back to bondage[52]

With only about fifty percent of eligible American voters actually casting their vote in a typical election, where would YOU place the USA on this cycle? Complacency? Apathy? Dependency? Obviously, approximately fifty percent of our citizens "depend" on someone else to make their decisions for them.

Edward Gibbons' classic *The Decline and Fall of the Roman Empire* described how Rome's decline began when the politicians discovered a new source of income. Instead of encouraging work, thrift, and savings, the leaders discovered that the political process could produce more money. They called the process taxation. The politicians raised wine prices, and then destroyed half of the orchards. This created the need for government subsidies, thus leading to a dependence on the government instead of on work and effort. The Roman government also created inflation to pay for its spending by debasing the currency, basically adding other metals into the gold and silver coins. The Roman emperor, Nero, said, "Tax, and tax again. See to it that no one owns anything." In 274 A.D., Nero became author of the first urban renewal program when he made welfare hereditary, a right, and an entitlement. Sounds familiar when we recognize that America's thirty plus year war on poverty has led us to have fourth generation welfare families. Only recently have conservative leaders pushed through welfare reform that has reduced welfare rolls in several states and restored dignity to people who went out and discovered that they *could* make it.

The Biblical work ethic—"if you don't work, you don't eat" —is the cornerstone of individual responsibility. The idea that an individual is responsible for where they are in life (self-government) is the same idea that has geometrically increased the wealth of the world. That is why it has been such a fight. Some people are just as dedicated to the idea that a huge government knows what's better for the individual than the individual knows for himself. Freedom isn't free. We have to understand that if we are going to be a free people we are always going to have to fight this fight. The fight today seems to be largely internal in the hearts and minds of the people of America.

Two prevailing types of philosophy, or government, have survived: free enterprise and communism. But you don't hear people talking about communism anymore. Those committed to a bigger government disguise their socialistic ideals by telling us how badly we need more government or more assistance. Frederic Bastiat wrote a pamphlet first published in June 1850 entitled *The Law*. Bastiat was a French economist, statesman and author who did a majority of his writing in the years that France was turning to complete socialism. He called taxation "legal plunder" and said that socialists "…desire to make the law their own weapon."[53] Bastiat went on to explain that "…legal plunder can be committed in an infinite number of ways… tariffs, protection, benefits, subsidies, encouragements, progressive taxation, public schools, guaranteed jobs, guaranteed profits, minimum wages, a right to relief, a right to the tools of labor, free credit… All of these plans as a whole-with their common aim of legal plunder—constitute socialism."[54]

North Korea, Cuba, and China openly flaunt their communism. An analysis of their economics and freedoms demonstrates some of their huge shortcomings: human-rights abuses and impoverished populations.

Each year, the Heritage Foundation publishes an *Index of Economic Freedom* that measures how well one hundred and fifty five countries score on a list of fifty independent variables that are separated into ten categories. Some examples of *Index* categories are: fiscal burden of government, government intervention in the economy, property rights, and regulation. The higher the score on a particular factor, the greater the level of government interference in the economy and thus, the less economic freedom that country enjoys. "The story that the Index continues to tell is that economically free countries tend to have higher per capita incomes than less free countries… the more economic freedom a country has the higher its per capita income is." Therefore, it is documented that the nations that limit government the most really do allow the people the greatest freedoms, the highest standards of living, and the most choices. In the *Index*, Russia, which has begun introducing free enterprise policies, is ranked 127 out of 155.

Cuba is at 152 and North Korea scores 155. China, despite the huge export of its own goods, still rates 114 because of its governmental intrusion.[55]

No system is perfect, but free enterprise is spreading all over the world. Today, free enterprise businesses flourish in countries where communism reigned a short time ago. Yet, while freedom grows around the world, too many socialistic practices thrive *here*. Thus, our fight now is internal, right here in our own country. It is better to trust the people than the government, but do enough of us understand and appreciate that?

If you love wealth better than liberty, the tranquility of servitude better than the animating contest of freedom, go home from us in peace. We ask not your counsels or your arms. May your chains set lightly upon you and may posterity forget that ye were our countrymen.

—Samuel Adams

Chapter 7

What Is the Alternative to Free Enterprise?

The alternative to free enterprise is summarized in a plan discovered in May, 1919 by allied occupation forces in Düsseldorf, Germany. It was first printed in the United States in the *Bartlesville (Oklahoma) Examiner-Enterprise* that same year. See if any of this rings true in America today.

The Communist Plan For Revolution

First of all, corrupt the young, get them away from religion, get them interested in sex, make them superficial, and destroy their ruggedness. Get control of all means of publicity. Get people's minds off of the government by focusing their attention on athletics, sexy books, plays, and other trivialities. Divide the people into hostile groups by constantly harping on controversial matters of no importance. Destroy the people's faith in their natural leaders by holding their leaders up to ridicule and contempt. Always preach true democracy but seize power as fast and as ruthlessly as possible. By encouraging govern-

ment extravagance, destroy its credit. Produce years of inflation with rising prices and general discontent. Incite unnecessary strikes in vital industries, encourage civil disorders and foster a lenient and soft attitude on the part of government toward such disorders. Cause the breakdown of old moral values: honesty, sobriety, self-restraint, faith in the pledge word, and ruggedness. And last, cause the registration of all firearms on some pretext with the view of confiscating them and leaving the people helpless.[56]

Even people who may disagree with the philosophies set forth in this book would agree that those "rules" largely have been enacted in the United States. Maybe it is just coincidence. But, perhaps there are people and philosophies that would use the freedoms our country provides to undermine us. Maybe there are still people who so hate our freedom and values that they have executed a plan to destroy those freedoms. Most have probably never read the main tenets of communism as listed in Marx's *Communist Manifesto*. I've listed the goals of communism below along with some examples of how they have already been at least partially enacted in our country.

Ten Goals of Communism from Marx's *Communist Manifesto*:

1.) Abolition of property in land and application of all rents or land to public purposes. (**Property taxes which, if not paid, allow government to confiscate the property.**)

2.) A heavy progressive or graduated income tax. (**Personal income tax rates in the United States had risen to as high as seventy percent until President Ronald Reagan cut** tax rates in the early 1980s. **Largest tax increase in American history was then enacted during President Bill Clinton's first term.)**

3.) Abolition of all right of inheritance. **(Inheritance taxes today penalize long-term commitment to work and success by taxing the surviving family after a business owner's passing. President George W. Bush lowered the inheritance tax rate in 2001 with the tax to be gradually reduced over time.)**

4.) Confiscation of the property of all emigrants and rebels. **(Rebels would be defined as any person or group so designated by those in power, conceivably being anyone refusing to agree with those in power. Examples would be government seizures, tax liens, IRS confiscation of personal property.)**

5.) Centralization of credit in the hands of the state, by means of a national bank with state capital and exclusive monopoly. **(Federal Reserve Board has broad power to determine interest rates and control the U.S. economy, exclusive monopolistic power to create and control money flow.)**

6.) Centralization of the means of communication and transport in the hands of the state. **(Federal Communications Commission determines licensing and regulation of those seeking communication access and the Federal Aviation Administration regulates the airline industry.)**

7.) Extension of factories and instruments of production owned by the state; the bringing into cultivation of wastelands, and the improvement of the soil generally in accordance with a common plan. (**Environmental Protection Agency has the power to condemn and confiscate lands as it deems necessary, also Departments of Labor, Commerce, Agriculture, Interior, and others formed for government influence in areas that could be kept private.**)

8.) Equal liability of all to labor. Establishment of industrial armies, especially for agriculture. (**Social Security administration, Department of Labor, assorted labor unions all seek equality in workplace and give the government the ability to affect the marketplace.**)

9.) Combination of agriculture with manufacturing industries; gradual abolition of the distinction between town and country, by a more equitable distribution of the population over the country. (**Corporate farms, regional planning and zoning laws, crop subsidies.**)

10.) Free education for all children in public schools. Abolition of children's factory labor in its present form. Combination of education with industrial production, etc., etc. (**Americans are taxed to support public education, controlled by the Department of Education which establishes curriculums, sets history standards, and generally decides what our school children are taught.**)[57]

Marx had it right when he observed that government intervention in the economy would lead to more government intervention. Ludwig von Mises, an economist and leading spokesman for individual liberties, proved the same point in his essay, "Middle-of-the-Road Policy Leads to Socialism." Mises demonstrated what Marx had only asserted: that state intervention (government interference) in the market place causes severe economic dislocations, which cause those adversely affected by the dislocations to petition the state for relief; when the state takes action designed to help those who suffered economically because of the earlier intervention, they cause further economic damage, which, in turn, spurs new calls for more intervention, and so on and so on, in a vicious circle that eventually ends in universal government control of all economic activity—in other words, in tyranny.[58] Ronald Reagan said in August, 1992, "We have long since discovered that nothing lasts longer than a temporary government program."[59]

Our government certainly serves a purpose, but it is scary that so much of our government resembles the original communistic framework for controlling people. The more frightening aspect is that more and more Americans look to government to solve their problems. As a contrast to the *Communist Manifesto*, I thought I'd include the "Ten Pillars of Economic Wisdom." These pillars were displayed prominently on the Hall of Free Enterprise at the 1964 New York World's Fair.

The Ten Pillars of Economic Wisdom

1. *Nothing in our material world can come from nowhere, nor can it be free: everything in our economic life has a source, a destination, and a cost that must be paid.*

2. *Government is never a source of goods. Everything produced is produced by the people, and everything that government gives to the people, it must first take from the people.*

3. The only valuable money that government has to spend is that money taxed or borrowed out of people's earnings. When government decides to spend more than it has thus received, that extra unearned money is created out of nothing, through the banks, and when spent, takes on value only by reducing the value of all money, savings and insurance.

4. In our modern exchange economy, all payroll and employment come from customers, and the only worthwhile job security is customer security; if there are no customers, there can be no payroll and no jobs.

5. Customer security can be achieved only by cooperating with management in doing things that win and hold customers. Job security, therefore, is a partnership problem that can be solved only in a spirit of understanding and cooperation.

6. Because wages are the principal cost of everything, widespread wage increases, without corresponding increases in production, simply increase the cost of everybody's living.

7. The greatest good for the greatest number means, in its material sense, the greatest goods for the greatest number, which, in turn, means the greatest productivity per worker.

8. All productivity is based on three factors: 1) natural resources, whose form, place and condition are changed by the expenditure of 2) human energy (both muscular and mental), with the aid of 3) tools.

9. *Tools are the only one of these three factors that humans can increase without limit, and tools come into being in a free society only when there is a reward for the temporary self-denial that people must practice, in order to channel part of their earnings away from purchases that produce immediate comfort and pleasure, and into new tools of production. Proper payment for the use of tools is essential to their creation.*

10. *The productivity of the tools—that is, the efficiency of the human energy applied in connection with their use—has always been highest in a competitive society in which the economic decisions are made by millions of progress-seeking individuals, rather than in a state-planned society in which those decisions are made by a handful of all-powerful people, regardless of how well-meaning, unselfish, sincere and intelligent those people may be.*

Already we do not live in a time of total liberty. What would our country be like if we just turned around some of these things that have impinged upon our liberties? What if we went to God's ten simple laws and those ten pillars of economic wisdom instead of having to deal with overly complex government laws: *i.e.* 10,766 pages of the Internal Revenue Code and some 150,000 pages of regulation to go along with it. What can we do to change these things? How do we become change agents and restore the foundation of our liberty?

The fundamental basis of this nation's law was given to Moses on the Mount. The fundamental basis of our Bill of Rights comes from the teachings we get from Exodus and St. Matthew, from Isaiah to St. Paul. I don't think we emphasize that enough these days. If we don't have the proper fundamental moral background, we will finally wind up with a totalitarian government which does not believe in rights for anybody except the state.

—Harry S. Truman

Chapter 8

Why Stand We Here Idle?

Each of us was born for a purpose. Not one of us is here by accident. It is an absolute miracle and a divine appointment, providentially decided, that you are reading this right now. We have a moral obligation and responsibility to pass the free enterprise message along to as many people as we possibly can. We need to have the attitude, "If it's to be, it's up to me." We all need to look at every opportunity as a commission to make a difference in as many lives as we can. What talents and assets have you been given that you've not fully explored?

When a good friend of mine, Charlie "Tremendous" Jones, encouraged me to write this book, I had several goals in mind. One was to impress upon people that America and the free enterprise system are special and did not come about by accident. Second, I wanted to convict people that if we become complacent, we will lose our precious freedoms and go the way of so many other societies. Third, I wanted to create in people a new passion for gaining knowledge about our history and direct them to more detailed sources that they can investigate further. Finally, I wanted to inspire people to become more involved and to truly participate in the arena of ideas. It is my prayer

71

that this book will inspire thousands of people to look around, find a need and fill it. Get involved in your community; be more active in your church; vote in every election; encourage every person in your sphere of influence to never miss an opportunity to vote; or maybe even start a business of your own. It is time that we as Americans decided to step off the sidelines and get in the game. We can no longer think, "Somebody will take care of this." Each American should look around and remember how blessed we are to live in the greatest country in the world with the greatest form of government in history.

No American will ever forget the terrorist attacks of September, 2001. Many of us got a frantic phone call from a friend or family member just in time to turn on the television and watch live as the second hijacked jet slammed into the World Trade Center. Those images are burned into our minds forever. The picture that made the most impact on me was of a lone fireman climbing *up* the stairwell in one of the Trade Towers as several other people filed down past him. Some people run toward the challenge and others run away from it. Doing what it takes to make a difference often means you'll have to do the opposite of what the crowd is doing. It may even mean doing what you don't really feel like doing at all. You may have to go against the flow. That's okay. Just realize that most people will seek the easy way. The ones who make a difference seek the right way.

Michelle and I recently saw a little-publicized film called *Pay It Forward* (based on the novel by Catherine Ryan Hyde) in which a seventh grade social studies teacher gives his class a year-long assignment to go out and make a difference in the world. Most of the students do the predictable: pick up trash, clean up graffiti, help an elderly person cross the street. But one boy decided to pick three people and do something for them that they could not or would not do for themselves. He drew the concept out on the chalkboard and called it "Pay it Forward." The idea was that when he did something for each of the three people he picked, they had to pay the favor *forward* (as opposed to paying it *back*) and pick three people that *they* would do something for. The boy's vision was that if each person just picked three people to unselfishly help, the idea would perpetuate itself and the world would be a better place. He had it right. We could all make a difference if we just decided to pay it forward. All it takes is a decision. What is your cause? What could you do to make a difference?

The Biblical story of Esther is a legendary account of someone called to make a difference at a particular place and time for her people. Esther didn't realize it, but she was uniquely positioned to do something that no one else could do. A wicked man named Haman, the king's right hand man, was very jealous of the Jewish people. He decided to convince the king that all Jews must die. The queen happened to be a young Jewish girl named Esther, but no one in the palace knew her ethnicity. Her Uncle Mordecai discovered Haman's plot and exhorted Queen Esther to risk her life by petitioning the king on behalf of the Jewish people. In Esther 4:14 He said, "Who knows but that we have come to the kingdom for such a time as this?"

This is the question that keeps coming to me as I work to make a difference. Now I'll ask you: Who knows but YOU have come to this hour for such a time as this? Who knows that he/she has been appointed at this time and this place and this point in history for a particular purpose?

Every generation has had some patriots who were willing to stand in the gap and do their part to keep free enterprise alive. Now it is our turn. Just think-history is full of stories of one person stepping up and making a difference. What are you passionate about? What is an area that you care enough about to get involved and be the change agent who makes the difference?

There is a seed of greatness in each of us. Maybe you had an idea for an invention when you were just a teenager and it has lain dormant for decades. Maybe you have a business or philanthropy idea that you have neglected to pursue because you were afraid others would cut it down or you couldn't get the financial backing you needed. Dare to dream. Dare to step out of mediocrity into a life of adventure. Keep the security of your job for a while, moonlight with your idea. When you build up enough confidence, be willing to risk it all to go for your dream. Most die with their dream still left inside of them. It's better to have risked and lost than to have never tried. You may have missed out on an opportunity that could have changed the world. Don't laugh at the band-aid, the post-it note, Federal Express, and McDonald's. They changed the world we live in. You can do that too. Pull out from your gut what is great about you. Then you will be able to bring out what is great in others. Entrepreneurship is what makes our nation great. People from all over the world come to America to make their dreams come true. Why shouldn't Americans dream again? Thousands of people have died in the last 225 years for this idea called freedom that gives us the right to pursue our dreams. Don't waste it. Why not you? Why not now?

Patrick Henry said it best in March, 1775 when he gave what is now recognized as one of the greatest political speeches in American history:

For my own part I consider it as nothing less than a question of freedom or slavery... It is only in this way that we can hope to arrive at truth, and fulfill the great responsibility which we hold to God and our country... If we wish to be free; if we mean to preserve inviolate those inestimable privileges for which we have been so long contending; if we mean not basely to abandon the noble struggle in which we have so long engaged; ...we must fight... An appeal to arms and to the God of Hosts is all that is left us! ...when shall we be stronger? Will it be next week, or the next year? ...Shall we gather strength by irresolution and inaction? Shall we acquire the means of effectual resistance by lying supinely on our backs, and hugging the delusive phantom of hope, until our enemies shall have bound us hand and foot? Besides, we shall not fight our battle alone. There is a just God who presides over the destinies of nations; and who will raise up friends to fight our battle for us. The battle is not to the strong alone; it is to the vigilant, the active, the brave... Gentlemen may cry peace, peace, but there is no peace. The war is actually begun. The next gale that sweeps from the north will bring to our ears the clash of resounding arms. Our brethren are already in the field. Why stand we here idle? Is life so dear, or peace so sweet, as to be purchased at the price of chains and slavery? Forbid it, Almighty God! I know not what course others may take; but as for me, give me liberty or give me death.[60]

Patrick Henry has a message for us today. Read his words carefully-again-and consider where you are right now. We who hear this call are the vigilant, the active and the brave. The war HAS already begun. Some of our brethren ARE already in the field. The forces that mass against free enterprise are active right now doing their best to undermine our heritage. Socialism and its close cousins have made startling advancements into our culture. But it's not too late. If free enterprise-loving Americans decide to not stand by idle, we can and will make a difference.

Letter to the Editor

A sample letter to use when responding to news items that misconstue the concept of "separation of church and state."

Dear Sir:

Recent editorial

I read with interest your recent (letter from _____, editorial) regarding the (First Amendment, separation of church and state, religious background of America's Founding Fathers).

Anyone making statements that our Founding Fathers were not predominantly Christian, or that they did not base our form of government on God's eternal laws, or that they intended the form of "separation of church and state" that we have today, is sadly mistaken. A small amount of homework conclusively reveals otherwise. Just a few truths for your study: The University of Houston conducted a study in which 15,000 writings of the founders were assembled. The fathers quoted John Locke, Montesquieu, and Sir William Blackstone, but they quoted the Bible four times more that any other source. In reference to the phrase "separation of church and state," one can easily discover that, not only were these words taken out of context, but Thomas Jefferson, who is credited with that statement, was not even present at the session in which the First Amendment was discussed and written. In court proceedings, hearsay is not allowed as admissible evidence. Surely, you would have to admit that statements made by someone not present at the discussion would be classified as hearsay.

Check it out for yourself. Start with www.WallBuilders.com or www.FreedomTide.com and go from there. Pick up any pre-revision history book. I am sorry that our current curriculum designed by revisionists no longer teaches the truth, but that does not mean that we as Americans have to plod along like cattle, just following some ill-advised lead. A friend of mine says, "It is okay to be honestly mistaken, but once one has been presented with the truth, that person either ceases to be mistaken or ceases to be honest."

Respectfully,

Notes

In a book of this size, I can only begin to scratch the surface of this material. I encourage everyone to read some of the works cited in this section and learn more about America's true heritage.

1. William J. Bennett. The Devaluing of America (Colorado Springs, CO: Focus on the Family Publishing, 1992), preface.
2. Rabbi Daniel Lapin. America's Real War (Sisters, OR: Multnomah, 1999), p. 43.
3. Dan Rather, CBS News Anchor on the O'Reilly Factor television show, May 15, 2001, quoted in "Citizen Magazine" (Colorado Springs, CO: Focus on the Family, June 2001).
4. George W. Bush. Our Mission and Our Moment, President George W. Bush's Address to the Nation before a Joint Session of Congress, September 20, 2001, Newmarket Press, pp. 18-19.
5. Bill O'Reilly
6. Mayflower Compact. November 11, 1620, quoted in Marshall Foster, The American Covenant—The Untold Story (Thousand Oaks, CA: The Mayflower Institute, 1992), p. 86.
7. William Bradford. Of Plymouth Plantation, a new edition by Samuel Eliot Morison (New York: Alfred A. Knopf, 1997), p. 236.
8. John Jay. October 12, 1816. The Correspondence and Public Papers of John Jay, Henry P. Johnston, ed. (New York: Burt Franklin, 1970), Vol. IV, p. 393, quoted by David Barton, Original Intent (Aledo, TX: Wallbuilder Press, 1997), p. 334.
9. George Washington. September 19, 1796 in his "Farewell Address." Quoted by William J. Bennett, Our Sacred Honor (Nashville, TN: Broadman and Holman Publishers, 1997), p. 368.
10. Mark A. Beliles and Stephen K. McDowell. America's Providential History (Charlottesville, VA: Providence Foundation, 1989), p. 183.
11. Ibid, p. 184.
12. George Washington. "Proclamation: A National Thanksgiving," A Compilation of the Messages and Papers of the Presidents, 1789-1902, ed. James D. Richardson, 11 vols. (Washington, DC: Bureau of National Literature and Art, 1903), 1:64.
13. Noah Webster. 1832. Quoted in Bennett, Honor, pp. 397-398.
14. James Madison. 1778. Quoted in Beliles and McDowell, Providential History, p. 221.
15. Quoted in Willard Sterne Randall, Thomas Jefferson: A Life (New York: Henry Holt, 1993), p. 342.
16. Benjamin Franklin. June 28, 1787. Quoted in Bennett, Honor, p. 385.
17. George Washington. May 10, 1789, in addressing a Memorial from the General Convention of the United Baptist Churches of Virgina. John C. Fitzpatrick, ed., Writings of Washington from the Original Manuscript Sources, 1745-1799, 39 vols. (Washington, DC: U. S. Government Printing Office, 1932, Vol. XXX), p. 321.
18. Runkel v. Winemiller: 4 Harris & McHenry 276,288 (Supreme Court of Maryland, 1799).
19. Reports of Committees of the House of Representatives made during the First Session of the Thirty-Third Congress (Washington, DC: A.O.P. Nicholson, 1854), pp. 1, 6, 8-9. Quoted in Barton, Original Intent, p. 30.
20. Barton, Original Intent, p. 48.

21. Gary Demar. God and Government (Atlanta: American Vision Press, 1982), p. 163.

22. James Madison. June 8, 1789. The Debates and Proceedings in the Congress of the United States, 42 vols. (Washington, DC: Gales and Seaton, 1834-1856), 1:451.

23. Daniel Webster. December 22, 1820. Quoted in Beliles and McDowell, America's Providential History p. viii.

24. David Barton. The Myth of Separation (Aledo, TX: Wallbuilder Press, 1991), p. 46.

25. Robert B. Downs. Books That Changed The World, revised ed. (New York: Mentor Books, 1983), p. 325.

26. Baer v. Kolmorgen; 181 N.Y. S. 2d. 230 (Supreme Court NY 1958).

27. David Barton. America's Godly Heritage (Aledo, TX: Wallbuilder Press, 1990), p. 10.

28. United States Supreme Court. 1844, Vidal v. Girard's Executors; 43 U. S. 126, 172 (1844).

29. United States Supreme Court. 1892, Church of the Holy Trinity v. U. S; 143 U. S. 457 (1892).

30. Barton. America's Godly Heritage, p. 10.

31. United States Supreme Court. 1947, Everson v. Board of Education; 330 U. S. 1 (1947).

32. Justice Hugo Black. Ibid.

33. Barton. America's Godly Heritage, p. 13.

34. Thomas Jefferson. January 1, 1802 in a letter to the Danbury Baptist Association. Quoted in William J. Murray, Let Us Pray (New York: William Morrow & Co., 1995), p. 90.

35. William J. Federer. America's God and Country Encyclopedia of Quotations (Coppell, TX: Fame Publishing, 1994), p. 325.

36. James Madison. June 20, 1785. A Memorial and Remonstrance. Quoted in Charles Crisimier, Preserve Us a Nation (Gresham, OR: Vision House Publishing, 1994), p. 47.

37. Benjamin Rush. Letters of Benjamin Rush, L. H. Butterfield, ed., 2 vols. (Princeton, NJ: American Philosophical Society, 1951), 1:521, to Jeremy Belknap on July 13, 1789.

38. Wallace v. Jaffree; 472 U.S. 38, 107 (1984), Rehnquist, J. (dissenting).

39. Justice Hugo Black. United States Supreme Court. 1962. Engel v. Vitale. 370 U.S. 421 (1962).

40. Justice William O. Douglas. United States Supreme Court. 1962. Engel v. Vitale. 370 U.S. 421 (1962).

41. United States Supreme Court. 1963, Abington v. Schempp; 374 U. S. 203 (1963).

42. United States Supreme Court. 1980, Stone v. Graham; 449 U. S. 39 (1980).

43. George Washington. September 19, 1796 in his Farewell Address. Quoted in Bennett, Our Sacred Honor, p. 368.

44. Edwin Louis Cole. Treasure, (Southlake, TX: Watercolor Books, 2001), p. 8.

45. William Bennett. The Devaluing of America (Colorado Springs, CO: Focus on the Family Publishing, 1992), p. 21.

46. Walter E. Williams, in a speech at Hillsdale College in the March 2000 Center for Constructive Alternatives seminar, "Competition or Compulsion? The Market Economy vs. the New Social Engineering," reprinted by permission from "Imprimis," the monthly speech digest of Hillsdale College.

47. Balint Vazsonyi, <u>America's 30 Year War</u> (Washington, DC: Regnery, 1998), p. 179. Quoted in Tim LaHaye, <u>Mind Seige</u> (Nashville, TN: Word Publishing, 2000), p. 108.

48. Karl Marx and Frederich Engels, <u>The Communist Manifesto</u>, first published in English in 1848, this translation first published in 1888 by Samuel Moore, (Strand, London: Penguin Books, 1967), pp. 104-105.

49. Milton Friedman. <u>Free to Choose</u> (Orlando, FL: Harcourt, Brace & Co., 1980), p. 156.

50. John Eldredge. <u>Wild At Heart</u> (Nashville, TN: Thomas Nelson, 2001), p. 200.

51. Bob McEwen, "So That's How America Works," audio tape pack (Freedom Quest, Vol. 1). Freedom Quest International, 1996.

52. Quoted in "Mayflower Institute Journal," 23:4 (May, 2001).

53. Frederic Bastiat. <u>The Law</u>, (Irvington-on-Hudson, NY: The Foundation for Economic Education, 1994), p. 23.

54. <u>Ibid</u>., p. 22.

55. Gerald P. O'Driscoll, Jr., Kim R. Homes and Melanie Kirkpatrick. <u>2001 Index of Economic Freedom</u> (New York: Dow Jones & Company, 2001), pp. 1, 21-22.

56. "Communist Plan for Revolt," quoted on Chuck Baldwin website, www.ChuckBaldwinLive.com.

57. Karl Marx. <u>The Communist Manifesto</u>, 1848, quoted by Mark W. Hendrickson, <u>America's March Toward Communism</u>, (Spring Mills, PA: Libertarian Press, 1987), pp. 9-10.

58. Mark W. Hendrickson, <u>America's March Toward Communism</u> (Spring Mills, PA: Libertarian Press, 1987), P. 10.

59. Frederick J. Ryan, Jr. <u>Ronald Reagan: The Wisdom and Humor of the Great Communicator</u> (San Francisco: Collins Publishers, 1995), p. 57.

60. Patrick Henry, speech to Virginia Convention on March 23, 1775, quoted by David J. Vaughan, <u>Give Me Liberty: The Uncompromising Statesmanship of Patrick Henry</u>, (Elkton, MD: Highland Books, 1997), pp. 83-85.

About the Author

Chad Connelly is the Founder and President of the Freedom Tide Foundation, an organization committed to educating Americans about Free Enterprise and the foundational principles which have made America great. His foundation is dedicated to reestablishing those principles by inspiring and motivating individuals to get involved where they are and make a difference. Chad has spoken to thousands of people across America and in several foreign countries and is creating a groundswell movement of grassroots involvement in youth and adults alike.

Chad has a civil engineering degree from Clemson University and worked in the engineering field with a national consulting firm for over seven years before starting his own business. Since 1991, he has been involved in helping others start, run and become successful in businesses of their own. Each year he brings the message of free enterprise to thousands of people across the United States and has spoken internationally in Australia, New Zealand, Venezuela, and the Netherlands.

Chad and Michelle, his wife of 14 years, live in his home state of South Carolina with their two boys, CJ and Bennett.

If you believe in this message and in the importance of reestablishing free enterprise and Godly principles in America, you can invest in your own future and that of your children by helping us to expand and grow this message and ministry. Donations to the Freedom Tide Foundation may be sent to:

> Freedom Tide Foundation
> 1831 Wilson Road, PMB 154
> Newberry, South Carolina 29108-2921

Your comments and questions are welcome. We may be contacted by email at Orders@FreedomTide.com, and Chad may be contacted for speaking engagements by email at Chad@FreedomTide.com.